**brand**zeitgeist

Also by Chris Houchens...

- *A Marketer's Guide to HIPAA: Resources for Creating Effective and Compliant Marketing* (Foreword and Reviewer)

- *Achieving Customer Mindshare Through Advertising: Industry Leaders on Creating Awareness, Making a Lasting Impression, and Achieving Bottom-line Results* (Co-Author)

- *Blogging: Strategies for PR and Marketing Professionals* (Co-Author)

# **brand**zeitgeist

Embedding Brand Relationships
into the Collective Consciousness

*Chris Houchens*

iUniverse, Inc.
New York   Bloomington

**Brand Zeitgeist**
**Embedding Brand Relationships into**
**the Collective Consciousness**

*The views expressed in this work are solely those of the author and do not necessarily reflect the views of the publisher, and the publisher hereby disclaims any responsibility for them.*

*iUniverse books may be ordered through booksellers or by contacting:*

*iUniverse*
*1663 Liberty Drive*
*Bloomington, IN 47403*
*www.iuniverse.com*
*1-800-Authors (1-800-288-4677)*

*Because of the dynamic nature of the Internet, any Web addresses or links contained in this book may have changed since publication and may no longer be valid.*

*ISBN: 978-1-4502-0679-2 (sc)*
*ISBN: 978-1-4502-0681-5 (dj)*
*ISBN: 978-1-4502-0680-8 (ebk)*

*Printed in the United States of America*

*iUniverse rev. date: 1/26/2010*

For Jackson and Alana

"*What I say today everybody will say tomorrow, though they will not remember who put it into their heads. Indeed they will be right for I never remember who puts things into my head; it is the Zeitgeist.*"

--George Bernard Shaw

# Contents

# Preface

This book will not solve your current marketing problem. However, it might help to stem marketing problems that could present themselves a few years down the road.

The truth is there are many companies who are utilizing shortsighted marketing schemes that will just get customers in the door to meet this week's sales quota. They are neglecting the customer relationships they could be building for success next week, next quarter, or next year. They're focusing on the short-term with their marketing and killing their long-term success.

Smart companies know the most effective marketing strategy is to build a long-term relationship with a dedicated group of customers. This is better known as branding.

What this book attempts to do is clarify how a healthy brand image is the most important marketing tool an organization can have. It explains how a long-term systemic branding philosophy can help make the other aspects of marketing easier and cheaper. It shows how a strong brand nourishes a current customer base and helps develop new customers.

The book uses the concept of the zeitgeist, the public's collective consciousness, as the framework to use to integrate a brand into a specific market.

This book is offered as a guide for developing an overall brand strategy and brand philosophy, not to offer a playbook of specific marketing tactics. Think of this book as a basic guide for your overall nutritional plan rather than what you should have for lunch.

Branding is a big-picture view of business. The zeitgeist is a big picture view of what the public is thinking about. When you combine these two large-scale visions and make connections between them, you can develop penetrating marketing tactics that will be successful with any target market.

# *Acknowledgments*

This book would not have been possible without Laura: my editor, my biggest fan, and my best friend.

# *Introduction*

In today's consumer focused world, brands encompass our lives. Between waking up and going to bed, consumers are met with a barrage of marketing messages. The challenge for marketers is how to make their brand stand out in this clutter.

We are also now living in an age when traditional forms of communication and marketing are no longer as effective as they once were. For years, marketers have been delivering interruptive marketing to a generic homogeneous mass market. As the market continues to segment itself into smaller and smaller niches, this method is becoming less effective in an increasingly crowded marketplace.

It's getting harder to get through and capture the mass market's attention. Consumers are increasingly blocking out irrelevant marketing messages and are instead choosing the messages in which they want to invest their time. With the aid of emerging technologies, consumers are also creating marketing messages. Branding is now a multi-dimensional conversation.

It's a challenging time for marketers. If companies continue to use traditional methods to reach consumers, then the chance for success is slim. However, if a business can embrace the new reality of marketing in a consumer-driven world, there's never been a better time for unbelievable growth.

In order to cut through the clutter and gain top-of-mind awareness with customers, you have to craft marketing messages consumers are willing to receive.

In order to have brand awareness spread virally among a target market, you must stake out territory in customers' lives.

You have to create dominant mindshare.

You have to create a Brand Zeitgeist.

# 1.

# What is the Zeitgeist?

Most people think they know what a brand is. (If you don't, you will by the end of the book.) But what's a zeitgeist?

The etymology of the word comes from the German words zeit, meaning time, and geist, meaning spirit, so the literal translation of zeitgeist is "the spirit of the times." A zeitgeist is the general intellectual, moral, and cultural climate of an era. In simpler terms, the zeitgeist is what is top-of-mind right now in the minds of any particular group. It's what people are thinking and talking about at any given moment in time.

Probably the most well known use of the zeitgeist concept is Google's listing of its most frequent search queries. The Google Zeitgeist,[1] now part of the bigger Google Trends product, provides a good snapshot of what's on the public's mind as it shows what people are searching for online in any given timeframe. Google can show search trends over time and even a glimpse back to see what people were thinking about in a certain time period.

In fact, Google can spot trends in the public zeitgeist so well that they can use the knowledge for other purposes. In the flu season of 2008/2009, Google tried projecting infectious disease trends with its search knowledge. They found they could beat the main flu map from the Centers for Disease Control as people would google flu-like symptoms and try to self diagnose long before they would see a medical professional who would then inform the CDC.[2] The success of the Google flu map shows that the public's search engine queries are a snapshot of what their concerns are and what's top-of-mind for them.

## Spotting the Zeitgeist

The zeitgeist goes beyond the Internet. The zeitgeist effect has always been present. A good indicator of a zeitgeist is any topic that you could walk up to a complete stranger and start discussing and they would know what you were talking about. From soft topics like a national sports championship game or "Who shot J.R.?" to major issues like the September 11th attacks or the Kennedy assassination, the zeitgeist is subject matter that is currently significant for the majority of people in a given group.

The size of that group is dependent on the topic and what they consider important. Even as the masses increasingly become more segmented, you can still sometimes see a national and a global consciousness. As technology makes it easier for like-minded individuals to communicate with each other, you see smaller niches with their own zeitgeists.

The time frame is important when referencing a zeitgeist. Looking back in time, we can clearly delineate major macro-zeitgeist periods and the mindset of the entire culture at those times. The farther we look back, the more time we clump into these zeitgeist periods. We can see very long epochs of civilization like the Stone Age or the Bronze Age. Our present culture has organized time into shorter past periods like the Victorian Era or the Renaissance where we see that large pockets of civilization possessed a certain mindset.

When we look more recently in retrospect, some of the most commonly defined zeitgeists are the decades of the twentieth century. Even if you didn't live through the Roaring 1920s, the counterculture era of the late 1960s, or the dot-com era of the 1990s, your mind's eye can probably conjure the stereotypical image of the zeitgeist in each of those periods from a Jazz Age flapper dancing the Charleston to a hippie putting flowers in her hair on the corner of Haight-Ashbury.

The most difficult large-scale zeitgeist to define is the one we're sitting in. Just as the people who lived in the Renaissance didn't fully recognize they were living through the rebirth of Western culture, we are unable to see how a future society will define us when they have a clearer picture of everything we did. While it's impractical to try to define our existing zeitgeist position on a long-term level, it's also tricky to define the short-term quick lived micro zeitgeists because those are constantly evolving faster as we become more plugged in.

A current short-term micro zeitgeist can go away as quickly as it appeared. What's hot today may not be hot tomorrow. From the water cooler talk about last night's big TV event that will fade by the end of the day to an election cycle that lasts several months, there are many zeitgeists occurring for any defined time period. The micro zeitgeist is always changing from year to year and day to day and increasingly from moment to moment.

## Spreading the Zeitgeist

The more instantaneous that the communication method can be delivered and spread, the faster these short term zeitgeists can change and evolve. It took a while to spread the message of Revolution in America in the late eighteenth century or to spread propaganda in the Second World War. Today, an internet meme can be forwarded around the world or an idea re-tweeted almost instantaneously.

As technology has made it easier for the zeitgeist to spread, it's also made it easier to switch to another point of focus. Trends on web aggregators like Digg or Reddit and what's hot on Twitter or Facebook change several times a day. The zeitgeist focus is there for a few moments, and then it's on to the next thing.

Since the advent of mass media, zeitgeists have increasingly followed the public's consumption of media. From Gutenberg's printing press to forwarding an email, zeitgeists are primarily defined and spread by technology and media.

Today's pop culture and the 24-hour news cycle provide the country with a prompt of what the zeitgeist should be for the day. Pick up a newspaper, turn on the TV, or log onto the Internet, and you'll see today's media-defined zeitgeist. This politician is involved in a scandal. That corporation is having financial difficulties. This storm or other natural disaster is influencing this area. That celebrity has done something outrageous. It's something different everyday.

While still dominant, the traditional mass media defined zeitgeist is starting to break down. Previously, a select group of editors at a few wire services and national networks decided what the zeitgeist topics would be by choosing the topics that would be pushed to the public. As technology develops where media becomes more of a pull technique rather than the old push method and end users create their own individualized information packages, it causes the main zeitgeists to fragment into numerous mini zeitgeists for niche groups.

## Zeitgeists are important in marketing

So, again in simple terms, the zeitgeist is what's on people's minds. But what does this zeitgeist concept have to do with branding and marketing a product?

It comes down to two things. Of paramount importance is having your product be on the forefront of the consumer's mind as they interact daily with the zeitgeist. In addition, it's important that your present customers be able to spread the word into the zeitgeist about your product through word-of-mouth and other viral channels.

The key to both of those issues is for your brand to have a zeitgeist quality. A solidly built brand with a good product will have a natural zeitgeist quality to it that people will want to share in their personal social networks. The question is how to develop that great brand, how to tell people about it, and then how to maintain that customer relationship. However, before you can establish a brand in the zeitgeist, you have to understand what a brand really is.

# 2.

# What is a Brand?

Branding is one of the most misunderstood aspects of marketing. It's become a passé buzzword that has completely lost the respect it deserves.

One of the reasons for the misunderstanding is that many people don't fully realize the true concept of brand. Most of the time, the understanding only goes skin deep to the brand's visual aesthetics. While visual and tactile representations like logos and colors are important, the real significance of a brand is not something that can been seen or touched.

## Brands are relationships

At its most basic, a brand is a relationship between something and an individual. A brand is a promise that past performance will be an indicator of future results. A brand is shaped by a customer's positive and negative interactions with the brand. You might see a brand as something only related to a company or other structured organization. However, anything can be a brand: a product, a service, an experience, a person.

A brand has a personality. People choose brands as they choose their friends: those that align with their own worldview, share the same values, and match their personality. The most successful brands are like trusted friends.

You can take the analogy too far, but looking for brands to trust is a lot like finding people you can trust and depend on. Just as when a friend breaks a promise or betrays trust and it damages the relationship, so it is with brands. I'm sure you've been angry with companies just as you have been with people. You may threaten to break off a friendship with the person, or you may threaten to never do business with a company again.

Your brand is your most powerful asset, but it's also an asset that you don't really own. Branding is not developed from the top down. It's developed from the bottom up. The consumer, not the company, dictates what the brand image is for any product. The frustrating reality of branding is that while you can provide the tools and platforms of a brand strategy, the brand actually exists only in the minds of the public, the same as the zeitgeist.

A brand is what people think about you, which is something you'll never fully be able to control. You can't own a brand. You can only manage it.

A brand is not something that can be built; it can only be influenced with a strategy that projects how you'd like a given group to perceive you over the long term.

## Brand strategy is the core of marketing

Branding is not a short-term tactic. It is a long-term strategy. Brands don't develop overnight. It takes awhile both internally and externally for that image to sink in to the collective consciousness. As with any long-term strategy, minor adjustments can be made, but the master plan has to stay intact for it to work. The true characteristic of a good brand strategy is consistency over the long-term.

A good brand serves as the square-one bedrock for ALL the organization's marketing activities. A good analogy is the relationship between the U.S. Constitution and individual laws. Legislatures can pass laws, but those laws should not and cannot violate the basic rights and responsibilities that are laid out in the

Constitution. Just as you can implement a wide range of marketing activities, but none should conflict with the basic message of your brand strategy.

This connection between the brand and current marketing activities has a positive influence on the marketing return on investment (ROI). A strong brand makes other aspects of marketing cheaper and easier to do. If a brand image has been firmly established in the target market, then you don't have to spend money and time telling them the basics every time you communicate with the target market. For example: Kentucky Fried Chicken (KFC) doesn't necessarily have to take time to explain the notion of the eleven herbs and spices in every ad because that concept is already ingrained within the brand. A good brand establishes basic groundwork that helps support and guide advertising, PR, and other marketing messages.

# 3.

## First Impressions Last

A successful brand is primarily a relationship between the brand and the market, but brands are also visual. While the emotional and intangible part of the brand is of utmost importance, a well-developed brand strategy needs a clear visual distinctiveness with logos, colors, fonts, and overall marketing tone.

In general, the way you look says something. The clothes you wear, the way you wear your hair, the accessories you carry; all of it gives the rest of the world hints about who you are, what your values are, and what they can expect from you. Brands are no different.

While logo does not equal brand, the logo is probably the preeminent visual aspect of a brand. A logo is the one item that should be consistently carried across all encounters that a potential target will have with the brand. An analogy to keep in mind is that a logo is like a person's face and the brand is like their personality. People are recognized by their face, and they are interacted with through their personality.

Just as it might cause confusion among ones' friends if a person had facial reconstructive surgery or otherwise changed their look, confusion is also introduced when companies abruptly change their logos and identity package. Logos should be a long-term commitment and shouldn't radically change over the short term. Small imperceptible changes to a logo are the preferred method to keep the logo culturally relevant and timely across the long term.

## Logo does not equal brand

Logos are confused as brands all the time, primarily because they are the best way to quickly represent what the brand is. Businesses should take care to not to be caught in the "logo as brand" trap as the state of Kentucky did.

In 2004, the governor of the Commonwealth of Kentucky at the time, Ernie Fletcher, proposed that the state develop a unified brand strategy. The state was spending over $2 million a year for separate and overlapping marketing campaigns. Collateral pieces from all the different state agencies were incongruent. The stated goal of the brand strategy was to develop a unified and consistent image for economic development and tourism efforts.

The Commonwealth commissioned several different agencies to create spec pieces to support a brand identity package. Voting among the proposals was held online and at welcome centers, and the state eventually unveiled the winning Unbridled Spirit [3] logo and tagline.

*The Unbridled Spirit logo for the Commonwealth of Kentucky*

Kentucky took a great and badly needed first step by sending out a unified and consistent message with Unbridled Spirit. However, the state government kept saying that the new logo was the new Kentucky brand. That is incorrect. Unbridled Spirit is a just a logo with a tagline, not a brand.

The Kentucky brand is built each day when the state is depicted in media, when Kentucky's citizens visit other states, or when people visit Kentucky. What those non-natives think about the state makes up the Kentucky brand — which probably currently consists of horseracing and the negative connotations of Appalachia. Fried chicken ranks up there, too.

The truth is that each U.S. state already has a brand, but not all have logos. Think for a moment about other states. You have developed an individual brand for each of them in your mind. For me, Alaska is cold, wild, and rugged. Iowa is flat and full of corn. Idaho has lots of potatoes. Arizona is a desert. There is a lot more to each of these states than those quick impressions, but those are the ones that are in the forefront of the nation's zeitgeist.

Has Unbridled Spirit affected the brand image of Kentucky? While the logo by itself probably had little effect, marketing campaigns using the logo have increased positive brand perceptions of the state including the horse industry and natural features.

The effort did clearly accomplish one of the goals. The marketing campaigns and collateral pieces from the state now have a somewhat unified and consistent image. There is now always a mandatory awkwardly placed Unbridled Spirit logo somewhere on everything that state dollars have funded just to make sure they're getting their money's worth.

## Visuals go beyond the logo

The way you present your other marketing activities is also a tangible representation of the brand. The tone of pieces like ads, brochures, press releases, and web site design reflect the personality of a brand just as clothing styles represent the personality of a person. Is the tone of your marketing casual and conversational denoting you are a friendly company? A more formal tone conveys more gravitas, responsibility, and security. A bank doesn't need to use the font Comic Sans in its marketing while a carwash doesn't need to use the colors gray or black in theirs. Make sure your tone matches your brand strategy and then make sure it's consistent across all communications you have with the market.

Colors telegraph much about a brand. Make sure the colors that you use in your business match the brand image that you want to convey. Red is passionate and dramatic. Yellow is cheerful. Blue is calming. Bright pastels are trendy. Black is powerful. Earth tones transmit an organic attitude. White feels pure. Gray has an urban quality.

A problem many companies have is that they develop the visual identity package before developing the brand strategy. Look at what you're attempting to suggest with the brand first and then build that into the visuals. Remember that the colors, packaging, and general look of your product and marketing oftentimes are the first encounter that consumers have with your product, and first impressions last.

An early 20th century marketer named Louis Cheskin coined a concept called sensation transference. Cheskin said when people assess a potential purchase; they transfer the impression of the colors, packaging, and other looks to the product itself. Basically, Cheskin says that consumers don't really make a distinction, on a conscious or subconscious level, between the visual representation of the brand and the product itself.[4]

In Malcolm Gladwell's book, *Blink*, he relates the story of how sensation transference affected customer's brand perception of Seven-Up when the soda maker changed their packaging…

> "We tested Seven-Up. We had several versions, and what we found is that if you add fifteen percent more yellow to the green on the package — if you take this green and add more yellow — what people report is that the taste experience has a lot more lime or lemon flavor. And people were upset. 'You are changing my Seven-Up! Don't do a 'New Coke' on me.' It's exactly the same product, but a different set of sensations have been transferred from the bottle, which in this case isn't necessarily a good thing." [5]

Tropicana orange juice had a similar reaction from their consumers when they changed their packaging and visual identity as a part of Pepsico's massive rebranding sweep in early 2009.[6] Tropicana dropped their well-established logo and an iconic image of a straw in an orange in favor of a more minimalist and modern look. The company was flooded with consumer complaints and online protests were organized against the company. The company relented and went back to the old look.

*Tropicana orange juice attempted to change their visual identity*

You might argue that people just don't like change. However, basic change is not what consumers fight. It's the perception that you're changing the relationship. During the same rebranding sweep at Pepsico, the visual identities of Pepsi, Mountain Dew, and other brands were also changed with little negative consumer feedback. It goes back to the core branding tenant that branding is not about the look; it's about the relationship. The Tropicana consumers apparently had more of a relationship with the visual aspects of Tropicana than drinkers of the other Pepsico brands did.

Even what could be conceived as small imperceptible changes to core assets of the brand can cause a consumer backlash. In the summer of 2009, IKEA changed the font they used from their signature typeface, a customized version of Futura, to Verdana, a font that they felt would be more functional and easier to read.[7]

At first glance, it might seem like an inconsequential move. However, you have to think about the mindset of a hardcore IKEA consumer, a person who is mindful of unique and modern design. Many of these customers said they felt betrayed in their relationship with IKEA with the font change. They reckoned that if the unique design of the font was something that could change, could the unique design of the products also eventually change?

It's all about the brand relationship. Thinking back to the analogy of brands and people's personalities, what if your spouse who had had the same look for years suddenly started dressing differently or acting differently? Would that trigger a response of concern from you? Why are they changing? What else could change?

## Rebranding is usually a bad idea

One of the keys for a company that wants to generate a zeitgeist brand is to fight the temptation to "freshen up the brand" or to "rebrand." When you think your brand images are getting stale, they've barely registered to the public. When you're sick of your branding efforts, they've just started to sink in. When your brand assets have been used for decades, you are established. Consumers become comfortable with the way a brand looks. Changes make them uncomfortable.

Imagine spending years investing money into a home mortgage. Suddenly, you become tired of the old house and just abandon it. You purchase a new house and assume a new mortgage with no equity brought forward from the old one.

Rebranding does the same thing to your brand. When you carelessly rebrand without forethought, you lose all the brand equity you've built up and have to start fresh each time.

One of the industries that continuously has some of the worst examples of throwing away brand equity is radio broadcasting. Radio stations spend an amazing amount of capital to build a loyal audience of listeners and advertisers only to abandon them in favor of a new format as trends change. In most media markets with all other factors being equal, you'll find that stations that have done a good job building a brand over several years do much better in ratings and ad revenue than those stations that are always chasing a new audience with a new format every few years.

Rebranding also fragments your customers' perceptions of you and makes it harder to control a unified zeitgeist effect. There will always be stragglers to your new image that still remember and relate to you in the old brand image.

Imagine that you move to a new city where you know no one and completely reinvent your personal image (you rebrand yourself). As you're interacting with your new friends who only know the "new" you, some old friends you haven't seen for awhile walk up and join the conversation. How do you interact with both groups and not betray the relationships and images that you have cultivated with each group? Rebranding causes the same awkward situation with the public as they attempt to interact with your brand.

## A matter of choice

Confronted with a plethora of choices, consumers will default to the one that they feel they have built a connection with, either on a conscious or subconscious level. That's why a brand is so important. The humbling thing for companies to remember about any brand, whether it is a product, service, experience, or a person, is that at the very basic levels, they are all incredibly similar and most would work for the consumers' needs. Differentiation of your product from similar ones is one of the major reasons to develop a brand strategy.

Think about fast food burgers. They're all beef patties between two pieces of bread. Nevertheless, I'll bet you prefer one chain's burger over another. Your preference may be due to the imaging efforts from the company or from your prior experiences with the chain, but that real or perceived difference that only exists in your mind is the essence of a brand.

## Doesn't taste the same without a brand

Probably the most famous example of removing the brand attributes for an unbiased product comparison is the Pepsi Challenge, an ongoing marketing promotion from Pepsi since the mid-1970s. The challenge is a blind taste test. Random consumers in public places sample two blank cups, one containing Pepsi and the other containing competitor Coca-Cola, and then are asked to pick which drink they prefer.

Pepsi contends that the results of the Challenge show more people prefer the taste of Pepsi to Coke. The challenge showcases that the public's preconceived brand perceptions of the public can and do override their own taste buds.

In fact, cola challenges even extend to the medical lab. Experiments have shown that patients with damage to the prefrontal cortex portion of the brain, which controls personality, decision-making, and social behavior, no longer have a brand-cued preference in cola choice.[8] It really is all in your head.

Alas, in the real world, you can't create controlled experiments to dupe the public into seeing their own prejudices. You have to work within the normal confines of a marketing campaign to defeat any negative preconceptions that are embedded in the zeitgeist.

It truly is a challenge for Pepsi. They have to continuously fight a perception battle. From the start, Coke has had many brand advantages over Pepsi including that Coca-Cola was the first real contender in the cola category and has become an inter-changeable term for cola for many people. So much so, that the following absurd conversation happens everyday in certain parts of the United States without either person blinking an eye:

"Do you want something to drink?"

"Sure, I'll take a coke."

"What kind?"

"A Pepsi."

For people in other regions of the country (the "pop" people) and especially for the cola companies, this exchange makes absolutely no sense. Nevertheless, it happens for the cola makers as well as for various other companies in different industries such as Kleenex, Xerox, and Google.

*Both Coke and Pepsi attempt to showcase their brand assets to reinforce brand identity while people are consuming their products.*

Both cola companies continuously fight a battle to differentiate their product. In the converse reality from the Challenge, both make sure that other visual and sensory attributes of the brand are showcased as people consume their product. From supplying restaurants with branded glassware to placing point-of-purchase signage in stores, both companies want their logos and colors to be associated with the taste. Both companies try to make sure people are drinking what they think they're drinking by mandating that restaurant servers correct patrons ordering a "coke" by responding with, "We serve Pepsi (or Coca-Cola), is that OK?"

The challenge to differentiate a product from similar competitors is a daunting prospect for any business, not just the cola giants. Companies invest massive amounts of time, energy, and money to make a product or service that they feel is superior to the competition. These brands expect that any rationally thinking consumer would see that their product is the best choice.

However, that's not the way it works. People don't always make sense. You can't just have a designer build a logo and suddenly have a brand that people recognize and can relate to. In order to create a brand zeitgeist, you have to get inside your customers' heads. You have to understand the mental state of not just one of your customers, but also the mindset of the public as a whole. You have to see the cultural trends that are shaping the perception of the masses. You have to use this knowledge to create that real or perceived superiority of your product in the minds of others.

# 4.

# Groupthink

A good marketer is a sociologist. In order to successfully sell anything to someone, you have to understand the economic, religious, political, educational, and other cultural nuances of the individual world in which that person lives. You have to craft marketing messages so that they are similar to the other types of messages that the person trusts and accepts from their social circle.

Sociology and other behavioral sciences are especially important in creating the brand zeitgeist. Understanding the fundamental ways that societies work and relate can help develop a brand strategy for a new product. That understanding can also help solve problems with existing brands when the public gets away from the core brand messages you're trying to communicate.

## The primal need

Humans have lived in organized groups for thousands of years. Anthropologists have discovered the earliest peoples in every civilization across the globe developed structured societies. This primal need to associate with like-minded people grew from fundamental needs such as food gathering and personal safety. In the same way that many of our other inborn primordial behaviors still manifest themselves in today's modern world, the need to be part of a group is still a deeply ingrained desire for humans.

In 1943, psychologist Abraham Maslow conceptualized in his "Theory of Human Motivation" that humans have a Hierarchy of Needs.[9] The most fundamental level of these needs includes basic physiological and biological requirements such as food, water, air, sex, shelter, and clothing. At the next level are the needs for safety and security. When these two basic levels of security and biological needs are met, a third level consisting of the need for acceptance and belonging emerges. This need primarily manifests itself as the need for friends and family, but also causes people to want be a part of a group.

The human craving to be a part of a group is so strong that it presents itself as a primary requirement in the hierarchy of needs, even before the needs of self-esteem or self-actualization. This is sadly exemplified in abusive relationships where a person stays in the relationship even though it damages their self-respect just because they want to be accepted.

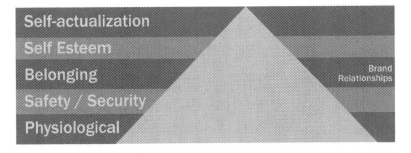

*The relationships that people have with brands and companies occupy the same space as the need for connections with family and friends.*

This dogged desire to have relationships with others is also the essence of what makes branding work. While the relationships people have with brands are, for the most part, secondary to relationships with other people, the affinity of the relationships is strong. Brands that have successfully built deep connections with customers seldom lose them because people have difficulty betraying the group relationship.

Brands build these connections when they are important in the customer's daily life. The brand that always wins is the one that has better top-of-mind awareness than its competitor. The way to get that dominant mindshare is to get involved in the customer's life and build a culture around the product. The brand images of companies such as Apple and Harley-Davidson are entwined into their customer's lifestyles.

Some brands complain that they can't build a consumer culture around their product because it's too mundane. How can users get excited about everyday items like toothpaste or tomato sauce? Commonplace items are perhaps the best products to build a culture around, because they're purchased often and used everyday in the person's life. This can help create a brand habit much easier than a big-ticket purchase that happens every few years.

Remember that there are other people involved as well. The brand relationship goes beyond a binary connection between the product and the consumer. A brand zeitgeist not only consists of the relationship with the brand, but also lets users have a bond with other users of the product. Chicago Cubs fans are devoted to their team so they also can empathize with other fans of the team during good and bad times. Deadheads not only followed the Grateful Dead across the country, but also built a culture with other fans. Members of political parties can identify with others who share their political ideologies.

## Unwritten Rules

Just as the zeitgeist works on the macro and micro levels, groups do as well. While it's easy to define societies based upon large-scale geo-political, ethnic, or other similar cultural identities, a micro society can be built with just two people. Whether it's the combined patriotism of the people of the United States or Robinson Crusoe and Friday battling the savages, groups emerge from common experiences, shared goals, and mutual threats.

It's easy to find these micro-societies tucked into the macro ones. While U.S. citizens think of themselves as Americans, they are also Texans, Kentuckians, Californians, or other state residents. Each of those states has other microcosmic groups within it from counties to cities and even right down to the neighborhood level. Each of those levels of assemblage carries its own unique identity of what it means to be a member of that group.

Group identity and membership go well beyond just geographic lines. Think about the different cliques in a high school or the different departments inside a company. Whether it is the jocks and the nerds inside the school or the company's accountants and IT technicians, each one of the groups has their own unwritten rules on the way to dress, act, and relate with each other and outsiders.

The common shared experiences of any group of people affect their perception and worldview. You can see the cultural connections more easily when a faction of people have separated and evolved a bit differently than their mainstream parent group. The people of Hawaii are as American as anyone from the other forty-nine states, but they have one slight difference.

The residents of the state of Hawaii as well as some other U.S. territories in the Pacific consume more SPAM per capita than any other place in America. SPAM is served at McDonalds in Hawaii. Hawaiian pizza parlors offer SPAM as a topping. A dish that is similar to sushi called SPAM musubi where cooked SPAM is combined with rice and wrapped in seaweed is also very popular.

*Hawaiian residents consume more SPAM per capita*
*than any other place in America.*

Why? It was difficult to get fresh meat to soldiers fighting in the Pacific theater during World War II. Since SPAM was shelf stable and could easily be shipped in to troops, GIs ate massive amounts of SPAM, as did natives of the islands. After the war was over, the island people continued eating SPAM. The current residents of Hawaii have never known a world where SPAM was not just another mundane fact of life. The perception of SPAM in Hawaii is very different from that on the U.S. mainland. [10]

Marketers should remember that there are groups with slightly different worldviews throughout any given society. Making sure the brand and the brand message relates to each of those unique worldviews helps consumers relate to the brand.

## Generational Divisions

One of the most well defined and useful zeitgeist groups are generations. Clear zeitgeist lines can be drawn in these large swaths of the market. What makes these groups bind is that there is an overall shared experience of being shaped by the same cultural prompts while growing up in the same time period. There are currently four active generational groups in the United States. The group known as "Traditionals" were born before 1945. For the most part, they have a conservative outlook and value hard work and earning rewards. They look for meaning and satisfaction in life.

Baby Boomers were born between 1946 and 1964. They grew up in a time of dramatic social change in the United States. Boomers are competitive and optimistic while being concerned with self-improvement and advancement. They are the first (and last) generation that experienced a single national culture in the zeitgeist as mass media came into being with them and following generations segmented into niche groups.

Members of Generation X, sometimes dubbed as a dark horse generation, were born from 1965 to around 1978. Even though they were initially labeled slackers, Gen X now comprises a large portion of the workforce. They value a sense of belonging while maintaining their individualism.

Generation Y, also known as Millennials, were born between around 1979 to the late 1990s. They are the first digital native generation, having never lived in a world without computers. Millennials are similar to the Traditionals in that they look for meaning and satisfaction in life and value work-life balance.

Learning the idiosyncrasies of each of these generations is helpful in several disciplines such as human resources, but learning the habits, values, and outlook of each of these generations is especially helpful in marketing and branding. In general, each generation reacts to the previous one making alternating generations similar. Brands can look at how each generation will approach a situation and build marketing and brand messaging to match that generational worldview.

To create a brand zeitgeist, marketers have to understand and obey the unwritten rules of each level of every group (geographic, cultural, generational, et. al.) that their target markets are members of in order to establish and grow a brand. This takes research and constant refinement to match marketing efforts to those groups' collective consciousness.

The collective consciousness of a group is made up of the shared beliefs, values, traditions that act as a unifying force for any particular society. The concept of the zeitgeist, and the brand zeitgeist, is anchored in this idea of the collective consciousness. Learn how your market relates and communicates to one another and you can learn to communicate and relate your brand to the market.

## The crowd is not always wise

While you can use the inborn human grouping desire to build and develop a brand, groupthink and herd mentality can be dangerous. There have always been urban legends, myths, and rumors. Most are insignificant and pass without much impact. However, some cast dispersions on brands and have to be dealt with by the brand.

Communal reinforcement occurs when an idea is repeatedly asserted in a group of people, regardless of whether or not the facts are there to support the concept. After time has passed, the idea becomes a strong belief in people's minds and may be regarded as fact. Both the problem and the advantage of communal reinforcement is that it occurs whether the idea that is being spread in the zeitgeist is true or false.

There are hundreds of classic urban legends that are so well known that you can probably tell someone the story. Whether it's LSD on children's stickers, razor blades in Halloween apples, or worm meat in fast-food hamburgers, damaging falsehoods can be spread and believed through communal reinforcement.

There are also innocuous "facts" that are well cemented into the widespread zeitgeist that have no basis in truth: Eskimos don't have hundreds of words for snow. The rotational direction of water going down a toilet doesn't matter if you're in the Northern or Southern Hemisphere. Columbus was not the first European person to set foot in America. None of these is true, and they are, for the most part, harmless non-facts. However, the power of communal reinforcement can do real damage to brands.

In the early 1980s, multinational corporation Proctor and Gamble had to aggressively deal with an urban legend that associated its logo with Satanism. The logo, which had been in existence since the late 1800s, was said to contain many allusions to Satan such as the number of the beast, two horns of a false prophet, and other satanic symbolism. Concerned consumers spread the rumor and even enhanced it saying that they had seen the president of P&G appear on the Phil Donahue Show to declare his allegiance for Satan and that the company's profits were donated to the Church of Satan even though no such episode ever existed.

*An urban legend misleadingly said that a former logo of Proctor and Gamble contained references to Satanism.*

The P&G Satanism rumor and all of these other well documented cases of urban legends and myths were well established in the zeitgeist and spread using traditional off-line networks. The potential for false information about a brand is now exponentially worse with real time online networks.

When pop star Michael Jackson died unexpectedly in June of 2009, the initial news and commotion in the days following was still spread through traditional media and word-of-mouth. However, much of the talk surrounding the Jackson death and several other notable deaths in the infamous 2009 Celebrity Death Summer was also centered in new media spheres, particularly Twitter.

While digital user reports surrounding the deaths were nearly in real time and could be spread exponentially in a short time, many tweets and texts consisted of false information that was readily passed along by the next user. In the hours following Jackson's death, a bogus story about the death of actor Jeff Goldblum surfaced and spread. While one of the more prominent examples, the confusion and false reporting surrounding the Jackson death is not an isolated incident in social media. In many aspects, the transmission of news and information on real time networks has become mob rule especially for rapidly developing stories.

Brands need to be aware that the crowd is not always wise and be proactive in dealing with falsehoods in new media before they get out of hand. For example, in the 2008 presidential campaign, the Obama campaign had volunteers monitoring social media and reacting to evolving news.

Individuals want to trust and act on information given to them by their social groups. It's a confusing time for consumers as they have begun to distrust some of what they hear through their online networks. Everything is now viewed with a skeptical eye. Consumers are cynical and feel that any attempt by brands to enter their personal networks may be a malevolent effort. At the same time, there is also an opportunity for brands to use those same new media networks to create successful brand zeitgeists with authentic messages and the ability to quickly react to falsehoods.

## The need to believe

Using basic tenets of sociology and anthropology can help brands develop relationships with their markets by tapping into a more significant personal connection with consumers. Linking the brand to the cultural values and beliefs of the target market gives consumers a reason to find common ground with the brand and build a lasting relationship. These relationships are the building blocks of creating a brand zeitgeist. By sharing common cultural touch points, consumers can use brands as icons to represent what their personal identity is to the world.

A cup of Starbucks, a pair of Levis, and an Apple iPod are much more than just coffee, blue jeans, and a music player. They are examples of brands being used as symbols of particular lifestyles and each hold a meaning in the culture. They each unite a group of people, not by typical demographic markers, but by common unity in the use of the product to describe their lifestyle.

# 5.

## Trendsetters and Brand Evolution

As he taught and trained his young son on a backyard rink in Brantford, Ontario, Walter Gretzky relayed a piece of advice to the boy, Wayne, who would eventually grow up to become a hockey legend: "Skate to where the puck is going, not where it has been." [11]

Brands can take the same advice as they attempt to tap into the zeitgeist. After all, the essence of the zeitgeist is made up of current trends. Monitoring those trends, keeping a finger on the pulse of society, and making small brand adjustments are essential to keeping a brand fresh and relevant.

Predicting trends is hard. There is no crystal ball, but there is a key to the process. There is the old saying that those who do not learn from history are doomed to repeat it. It's a good lesson for brand managers as well. While technology, media, and communication methods are evolving faster than ever, fundamental human nature doesn't change that much. People will always be people and will always react in similar ways to similar events. For instance, excessive personal consumption in both the 1920s and 1990s predated economic falls in each of the following decades and consumers in each time period acted in a similar way before, during, and after each event.

At the same time that brands should attempt to stay close to the current cultural zeitgeist, there is a danger in watching and following trends too closely. It's important to understand the difference between trends and fads. A trend is the beginning of a long-term cultural shift whereas fads are short-term cultural distractions. The idea can be seen in a kitchen remodel in the 1970s. Hardwood flooring is still fashionable today; the avocado green refrigerator and range are not.

While it's hard to predict trends, it's even harder to tell the difference between trends and fads while in the midst of the zeitgeist. For example, in 1977, the CEO of Digital Equipment Corporation, Ken Olsen, told a gathering of the World Future Society that, "There is no reason for any individual to have a computer in his home."[12] While he wasn't specifically talking about what would become the modern day personal PC, the trend was clearly on the way. Conversely, an entire industry was temporarily created in 1999 around the Y2K bug that turned out to be a non-event. In retrospect, Y2K was a short-lived fad.

Brands that attempt to follow and match trends too closely will lose market perspective and become irrelevant. Two media examples of this phenomenon are the MTV and Saturday Night Live brands. Because of necessity in what each does, both brands have to hold tight to the current pop cultural zeitgeist.

Several times in the history of both SNL and MTV, each became unhip and passé, the converse of what their brand was supposed to embody. In each case, the programmers needed to kill off the old brand assets and resurrect as a new culturally relevant entity. While these media properties have been lucky enough to pull it off several times, so much so that reinvention every few years is almost now part of the brand, not all culturally disconnected brands have been as lucky.

Hummers and other types of large sports utility vehicles were a symbol of the suburban soccer mom zeitgeist of the late 1990s and early 2000s. While those types of vehicles were perfect fits for the spirit of the American big car culture at that time, when the zeitgeist suddenly shifted as gas prices spiked and the economy changed, automobile manufacturers were caught flat-footed. The auto brands and the cultural zeitgeist became out of sync.

In the end, two of the three major U.S. automakers, Chrysler and General Motors, resorted to bankruptcy while Ford reported its worst year in company history.[13] The entire auto industry was shaken to the core and had to reinvent and reposition their brands to reflect the new zeitgeist of the eco-conscious auto consumer.

## Smart Evolution

Since the culture and zeitgeist continue to change and evolve, brands must evolve as well but without losing sight of the brand's fundamental characteristics. It's important for a brand to evolve slowly and deliberately to keep pace with the market's ever-changing zeitgeist views. As mentioned in an earlier chapter, drastic changes cause damage to the brand-consumer relationship. Gradually fine-tuning the brand to match the market is preferable to a frantic pace of playing catch-up after realizing the brand and the market have grown apart.

Brands can maintain the equity they've built up if they execute their branding evolution correctly. The Old Spice brand of men's aftershave and other grooming products has been in existence since the mid-1930s. However, by the turn of the 21st century, the brand was not relevant to younger generations because they associated Old Spice with their fathers and grandfathers.

Old Spice de-emphasized their iconic white buoy shaped bottle while retaining the scent, logo, and other core brand assets. They added new products aimed at younger demographics such as body spray and shower gel, marketing these new products by capitalizing on the generation shift with taglines such as "The original. If your grandfather hadn't worn it, you wouldn't exist." [14]

*Old Spice is an example of successful brand evolution.*

Proctor and Gamble, the owner of Old Spice since 1990, successfully retained the brand's equity maintaining their current market of older men while concurrently introducing the brand to new generation of users. This was much more effective than a drastic re-branding shift.

Sometimes the passage of time changes brands without any external input. Today, the brand image of Duncan Hines involves cake and other dessert mixes. However, prior to the 1950s, the zeitgeist revolving around the name Duncan Hines meant restaurant reviews. The real Duncan Hines was a traveling salesman from Bowling Green, Kentucky. In a pre-interstate, pre-chain restaurant United States, he and other travelers relied on local eateries for meals. There was no way for a traveler to know if a particular local restaurant was any good. Hines began keeping a list of good places to eat in each town he visited and shared the list with others. His list became so popular that he published it as an annually updated book called "Adventures in Good Eating."

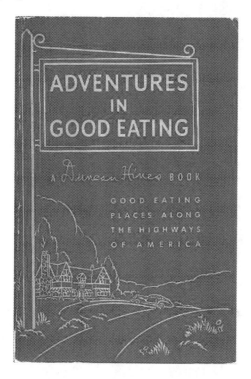

*In a previous zeitgeist period, the Duncan Hines brand meant restaurant reviews instead of cake mixes.*

Hines became one of the first modern food critics and was such a famous name in food that he was able to sell the rights to his name to a company that manufactured a line of cake mixes. After Hines' death in 1959, the cake mix with his name continued and the original meaning of the Duncan Hines' brand is now almost completely erased from the American zeitgeist. The meaning of the Duncan Hines' brand evolved as the attributes that people contributed to it changed.

The Duncan Hines brand is a case of positive natural evolution in the zeitgeist. The zeitgeist can also hijack a brand in negative ways. Prior to the advent of the Internet when someone mentioned spam, the canned meat probably came to mind. However, today the Hormel Foods Corporation is in a constant struggle to protect their brand.

Hormel is attempting to control the evolution of what spam means to the public. They don't object to people referring to unsolicited electronic mail as spam, but stipulate that it be spelled in lower case letters to distinguish it from their capitalized SPAM trademark. Hormel also objects to the use of their brand identity pieces such as the SPAM can and logo being used in relations to the electronic trash. Hormel also uses legal action against entities that attempt to trademark words containing spam. [15]

Brands will evolve over time because the zeitgeist evolves over time. It's up to the company to help guide the evolution or the zeitgeist will guide it for you.

## Looking beyond trends

While on the surface, it may seem like a smart move to match cultural trends tit for tat, brands work best when they are firmly grounded in something larger than trends. Just as people associate themselves with groups that are familiar to them and share similar values and beliefs, consumers will be more responsive to brands that have clearly defined and entrenched standards and principles.

When developing a brand strategy, companies should define the brand's core assets. Those core assets should reflect the unchangeable aspects of the brand. These core assets are analogous to the wedding vows of the brand-consumer relationship. They should be authentic, provide the reasoning behind why the brand exists, and should lay out the system of beliefs that the brand represents. This brand core should rarely be adjusted, if at all. It should be a reference point in every decision that is made and in every piece of communication from the brand.

While this idea of the brand core can seem overly academic and intense, the importance of the brand core can clearly be seen when it's violated. What if you sat down at a Ruth's Chris steakhouse and found bologna sandwiches on the menu? What if Abercrombie and Fitch started selling orthopedic shoes? What if PETA held a fundraiser at KFC? There's nothing wrong with bologna sandwiches, orthopedic shoes, or fried chicken, but those brands have core assets that are contrary to those products.

Customers and the general public have attributed a meaning to your brand. They have a connection to certain brand attributes. If you violate those core assets to keep up with trends, you've betrayed the relationship and there will be revolt. Brands cannot and should not try to be all things to all people.

Remember the discussion of the Pepsi Challenge? There's more to the story. In the mid 1980s, as Pepsi continued to promote that more of the blind taste testers preferred the sweeter taste of Pepsi, Coca-Cola decided to change one of its core assets and launched one of the biggest corporate blunders of all time. In taste tests, New Coke beat Pepsi but it almost destroyed the brand. Consumers felt the brand relationship had been betrayed. Eventually, Coca-Cola Classic was brought back and New Coke was quietly discarded. Looking back, we can clearly see that Coke reacted to the trend that was growing with the Challenge at the expense of their core assets.

When adjusting the brand to keep it culturally relevant, you should never betray long-term relationships for short-term gains.

## Watching from the sidelines is not an option

The term observer effect is used in the field of physics to describe the changes in outcome that merely watching an experiment will have. Anthropologists and zoologists have to be careful not to influence the behaviors in the tribes and groups they are observing. Star Trek fans understand the wisdom behind the Prime Directive. Brands also have to be aware they may be influencing the trends that they are watching.

One factor in the success of the Whole Foods brand is an increased awareness in the mainstream cultural zeitgeist to natural and organic products. This awareness is being driven by Whole Foods' customers, their competitors, the government, farmers, the media, and many others who are all providing input to the way the natural and organic cultural zeitgeist is being shaped. Because of their success, Whole Foods is also now both contributing to the organic/natural conversation and influencing the other players as well.

A brand that has been successful in creating a zeitgeist brand has to remember that they are now part of the trend equation. In fact, that level of brand influence is a marker of success. Good brands are following and leading their markets simultaneously. The brand should be continuously evolving because of input from the consumer, the brand, and external events in a never-ending cycle.

As an example, Twitter watches how its users use their micro blogging service and then centers the innovation and development of the service on user ideas. Several features at the heart of the service including the @username, re-tweets, and hashtags were developed not by the company, but by people using Twitter accounts.[16]

Giving such as high level of control over to customers can be hard for companies. Twitter originally didn't want their messages to be called tweets, but they now have trademarked the term.

One of the last things a cosmetics company wants is for people to use one of their products as bug spray. While resistant at first, Avon now embraces the idea that the public uses their Skin So Soft product in off label ways. So much so, that Avon now offers Skin So Soft insect repellant.

Brands that have reached the zeitgeist level will gradually be shaped less by the marketers and more by the consumer. Handing control over to the public is not a decision that will be made by the company. The users will determine the evolution. The smart company will help guide them.

# 6.

# First Things First

When setting out to achieve a brand zeitgeist, begin with a great product.

This seems like a given for any successful business — even if they don't have any brand strategy. Many companies inadvertently skip the important step of creating a great product or service that has a zeitgeist quality. It's not that these companies have inferior or bad products; it's that they just have an average product. Average is not notable.

Obviously, brands are looking for positive buzz as they encourage customers to engage in brand evangelism. If the product or service is remarkable, people will talk about it. If it's of poor quality or they have an awful experience with the brand, they'll certainly talk about it. However, average does not arouse passion in customers either way. Average certainly doesn't inspire the type of word-of-mouth marketing needed to introduce a brand into the public zeitgeist. The fact that average is not inspirational is a basic truth that has biblical roots:

> I know thy works, that thou art neither cold nor hot: I would thou wert cold or hot. So then because thou art lukewarm, and neither cold nor hot, I will spue thee out of my mouth.[17]

Being remarkable goes back to the ideas of consumers' social groups and trends. People want to share. They want to be the first to introduce new ideas to the groups they belong to and show they are keeping up with trends. No one is going to share average and mundane experiences. No one ever visited a restaurant and then recommended all their friends go there because the service was reasonable, the bread was OK, and the featured entrée tasted like chicken.

Many brands are stuck selling average products and providing typical middle-of-the-road service. Most are making money and nearly all have satisfied customers. What's wrong with that? Nothing until a competitor pops up and provides a slightly above average experience.

It's like a world where people have only eaten vanilla ice cream when suddenly someone shows up with a carton of chocolate. Generic brand loyalty is forgotten for the thrill of a unique new stimulus.

## Marketing is best built in, not slapped on

A few years ago, a national business magazine featured an article that detailed the steps needed to build a successful startup company. They listed developing the Sales and Marketing Plan as number 14 out of 16 steps.

That will never work. Marketing, and especially branding, should be thought of first because if no one buys the product all of the other steps were a waste of time. Brands should consider how marketing will interact with the product along each step of the product development process.

From the dawn of the modern consumer age until just recently, brands were created in one department and then taken to the marketing department to be marketed. However, if everyone worked together on simultaneous development of the product and the marketing, then the core attributes of the brand are a part of the marketing message and vice versa. Customers will be exposed to the marketing just by being a consumer of the brand. This builds and strengthens the brand relationship.

Involving the idea of the core brand from the beginning also helps the decision makers and employees at the company understand exactly what is being sold. Too many times, businesses can't see the forest for the trees. By continuously looking back at square one at each step in product development, businesses and employees can clearly see what doesn't belong and create concise and targeted products.

Southwest Airlines is a great example of how the brand and marketing message is a part of the product. In the airline business relationship, consumers pay for tickets to provide transportation from Point A to Point B. Southwest Airlines does a great job creating a unique brand experience with a mundane transaction. From flight attendants rapping safety instructions[18] to an industry disruptive business model that provides economical ticket prices, the Southwest brand is not just a logo and an airplane. Their customers expect a distinctive experience. Every employee knows what that experience is supposed to look like and strives to create it without having to ask permission from supervisors.

*The corporate culture and the experience of flying on Southwest Airlines is part of their brand.*

Marketing that is integrated into the brand goes well beyond the customer experience. It can also be embedded in the actual design, form, and function of the product. Dyson vacuum cleaners, Coca-Cola hourglass bottles, and Apple computers all embody strong aspects of their respective brands.

## A good name is rather to be chosen than great riches

In William Shakespeare's Romeo and Juliet, Juliet says, "What's in a name? That which we call a rose by any other name would smell as sweet."

While Shakespeare may not have a preference for naming flowers, there are preferences and best practices in the zeitgeist for the names of brands. Like the logo, the name of a product or business is easy shorthand to represent what the brand represents to an individual. Like the logo, the business name is a fundamental building block of the brand that all other marketing interactions rest on. Just as naming a child can either help or hinder the child for the rest of their life, business names carry just as much weight for success.

Avoid cute or funny names. The Curl up and Dye Hair Salon is only funny for a few times before it gets old.

You also need people to say and spell your name to make sure it can be communicated easily and without confusion across all mediums. Someone who heard a radio ad for the In Site Web Design Company may type Insight Web Design into their computer to find the business.

Try to be as descriptive in the name as possible to convey the brand image. I have no idea what the Epitome Corporation does, but I do have a hunch of what Epitome Architectural Services does.

Use that description in the name to build the brand. The businesses, Quickie Lube and Excellence Car Care Center will both change the oil in a car, but each name transmits a different image about pricing, clientele, and other brand characteristics.

The newest litmus test for brand names is the domain test. If a potential business name is already taken online, then another needs to be chosen. Trying to make a domain work is not a good idea either. For example, quickielube.com is what customers will probably type in when looking for the Quickie Lube. Using names like quickielubeonline.com or quickie-lube.com will require extra marketing effort and cost to communicate to customers and most likely that communication won't be 100% effective. It may be best to start with the domain search and build names off what web domains are available.

## It always starts at the beginning

After developing a unique and exciting product or service that has marketing built in, you are ready to introduce it to the public for them to take it into the zeitgeist. The key to introducing new brands into the zeitgeist is the product adoption curve.

The product adoption curve is a bell curve that charts when a consumer will start using a product for the first time. This curve slices the general public into five major groups:

Innovators represent about 3% of the population. They are well informed and up to date on existing trends. They are risk takers who are willing to try new experiences.

Early Adopters are well educated and make up about 12% of the populace. After careful consideration, they are also willing to try new things.

The Early Majority are cautious consumers who try new things after they have somewhat been proven by the previous two groups. They represent the first major portion of the curve with 35% of consumers.

The Late Majority also composes 35% of the population, but they are dubious consumers who acquire new items only after they have become part of the mainstream.

The remaining 15% are Laggards who are resistant to change and only adopt new products after all other alternatives are exhausted.

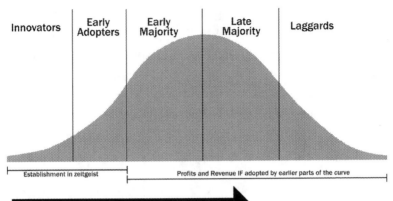

*It's important to establish a brand in the zeitgeist with
the early parts of the product adoption curve.*

A person may be in different groups for different product
categories. For instance, a consumer could be a laggard in technology but an innovator in trying new restaurants.

Videocassette recorders are an example of a recent product
that has gone all the way through the curve. Innovators and early
adopters bought VCRs in the late 1970s. The majorities bought
one in the 1980s and early 90s. The laggards got their first VCR
just a few years before DVD players became available.

In order for a brand to successfully enter the zeitgeist, you
have to firmly establish the brand with influential consumers in
the early parts of the product adoption curve, the innovators and
early adopters. Revenue and profits for brands come when the
product starts to be used by the majorities, but brands may never
get to that meaty part of the curve if they don't pass the hurdles
of the first two segments. The innovators are like the guinea pigs
for the early adopters. The early adopters are the "sneezers" who
introduce the idea to the bigger hunks of the curve.

Users in earlier segments of the curve are considered experts
by the participants who are further down the adoption curve and
will believe what those earlier consumers say. These authoritative

referrals will often overpower personal judgments or sometimes serve as a substitute judgment in lack of personal experience with the brand.

## I've never tried it, but I don't like it.

In early 2007, Microsoft introduced a new operating system named Windows Vista. The product was met with almost immediate hostile response from the technology community who said they had found many flaws and problems with the new system. Negative comments about Vista from a few influential online users then influenced other members of the technology world who also said they didn't like the new system. This perception from the computing world then trickled down and became a part of the zeitgeist of the general public.

*Negative perception in the zeitgeist hindered*
*Microsoft's marketing of Windows Vista.*

Whether Windows Vista was flawed or not became a moot point. There were reports of Vista users downgrading back to Windows XP as well as reports of users who said they planned to wait for the next version of Windows and skip Vista. In reaction to this change in the zeitgeist, many computer companies started offering to ship new computers with the older XP version rather than the new Vista system.

In all this bad publicity, the interesting thing surrounding the Vista launch at the larger general public level was that most of the people who said they didn't like the new operating system were people who had never actually used it. Microsoft saw that as an opportunity and launched a marketing campaign called the Mojave Experiment to combat the negative perceptions.

Microsoft invited people who had never used Windows Vista to rank their perception of the new operating system on a scale from zero to 10. Then, they were shown what they were told was Microsoft's new operating system called Windows Mojave. Participants were then asked to rank the new system on the same zero to 10 scale. After this, the subjects were told the truth; that Windows Mojave was just Windows Vista with a different name. The results of the experiment were staggering. [19] The average pre-session rating of Vista was 4.4 out of 10; while the average "Mojave" rating was 8.5 out of 10.

Even though the Mojave Experiment was criticized by many for not having accurate sampling and not addressing all of Vista's problems with those who participated, there are clear lessons about how the zeitgeist affects brand perception in early product development and rollout.

Prior experiences with a brand can be transferred to any new initiatives or products from the brand. This can be a good thing, as people will try new things from brands they already like. If people are fans of films made by a certain director, there's a good chance they will go see his new movie. On the other hand, negative experiences can also be conveyed forward. This is one of the things that led to the Vista problem. Even though Vista was a new product, Windows and Microsoft are well-established brands and some people have preconceived biases against the company. In the Vista instance, the problems snowballed.

Another lesson is that you can't change ideas that are firmly embedded in the zeitgeist. Even though Microsoft attempted to show that the public was prejudiced by preconceptions, the negative connotations of the brand were too much to shake. About two years after Vista was released, Microsoft introduced Windows 7 in October 2009 to positive feedback even though critics saw the new system as just a slightly improved version of Vista with a different name.[20]

The first steps in branding are the most important, but they're often the steps that businesses skip. Establishing a firm brand foundation with products/services that are buzz worthy, setting up strong basic brand building blocks like names and other brand identity pieces, and paying special attention to users in the early part of adoption curve can help make placing a brand out in the zeitgeist much easier and more successful. Those things are just the first step and won't necessarily work by themselves. The next step is telling people about the brand.

# 7.

## Brands are driven by the Message

After you develop a brand that people want to talk about and be loyal to, you have to introduce the brand to the consumer. You also want to give them the tools and knowledge to extend the brand out to the groups they belong to and then out to the overall zeitgeist. This is done through marketing messages like public relations, online efforts, and advertising.

Advertising and other types of consumer messaging are important parts of building a brand. Nevertheless, they're just a part of the overall brand puzzle. You cannot build a brand with just advertising. One of the biggest marketing misconceptions is that an ad campaign can establish a new brand or change perceptions of a current brand. The consumer creates brands. The company does not create them. Brands are a bottom up proposition, not top-down. Marketing messages like advertising are there to help guide this development in the consumer.

Brands are long-term relationships. A few ads over a couple of weeks are not going to change that relationship. Brands are developed over time by consumers' interactions with your organization. Advertising is an important consumer interaction. The goal of advertising and other marketing messages from the brand should be to guide and lead the development of the brand over the long term. Advertising's purpose is to reinforce a brand's position in the public's minds.

Advertising can be strong enough to enter the zeitgeist on its own merits. Some of the all time greatest brands still have their advertising messages embedded in the American zeitgeist. You know what brand of toilet paper that Mr. Whipple doesn't want you to squeeze, what credit card that you shouldn't leave home without, and what type of medicine goes "Plop Plop Fizz Fizz" because Charmin, American Express, and Alka-Seltzer spent plenty of ad dollars over many years to establish those concepts in the zeitgeist.

Hundreds of advertising jingles, taglines, slogans and mascots are still established in the zeitgeist even though their advertising campaigns stopped many years ago. Can those types of legendary ad campaigns be recreated today in a drastically different media and market landscape?

## The choice is yours

In the past, there were limited options in almost every consumer category. For any purchase, there might be two or three brand choices. It was relatively easy for brands to differentiate themselves from the competition and communicate that difference in their marketing message. With fewer media choices, brands could simply place their message in front of massive amounts of media consumers. With enough repetition of the message, it would eventually sink into the consumers' minds and they would recall it when standing in front of a store shelf.

Today both the shelves and the media marketplace are crowded and loud. Even simple purchases entail navigating through numerous brand competitors with hundreds of options across those brands. Not only are there more individual brands, but brands have introduced new brand extensions that cannibalize themselves.

Barry Schwartz opens his book, *The Paradox of Choice*, by describing the shelves of his local small supermarket being filled with, among other things: 85 varieties of crackers, 21 options for chocolate chip cookies, and 95 different types of chips. Schwartz makes the point in the book that in a world of increasing amounts of choices, even about simple things, consumers are forced to invest a progressively rising amount of time and energy to make decisions. It eventually rises to the level that they begin dreading the purchase interaction or suffer from buyers' remorse after the sale by second-guessing their decision. At some point, choices become debilitating rather than liberating.[21]

There are also increasing choices for both media placement and consumption. With advertisements on just three TV networks, a couple of radio stations, and a newspaper in each market, it was easy for marketers to make the right media buy and easy for consumers to digest. Now with hundreds of TV choices, a barrage of online ads, and billboards on every corner, the message is often lost or ignored.

## The keys to effective brand advertising

With today's constant bombardment of marketing messages and a fragmented media landscape, it's hard to insert ideas into the zeitgeist with advertising and PR. Effective branding through advertising must be clear, cut through the clutter, and help the consumer make the right choice.

The first key to effective advertising is a good ad. Seems like common sense, but there are plenty of ineffective creative pieces placed in media everyday. The main culprit contributing to this problem is that brands are trying to impress and entertain themselves rather than marketing to the consumer. Corporate marketing departments and ad agencies are often more concerned with creative execution and with winning awards than with delivering results. This happens more often with ads done in conjunction with branding efforts since those ads attempt to showcase intangibles.

All ads should sell the brand. Effective advertisements do two things at a minimum. They provide a reason for consumers to act by providing a unique selling proposition and they provide a call for that action. They can also be cleverly creative and win awards. However, if they don't contribute to the bottom line, they're useless, a waste of money, and oftentimes damaging to the brand. One of the biggest mistakes companies make is they think people pay as much attention to their marketing as they do. There are only two groups who actually want to see advertising: the people paying for the ads and the people who created the ads. The general public is not interested in advertising. They're interested in answers to their problems. Effective advertising does that by offering authentic messages that contain solutions to people's problems by using the brand.

Message authenticity is important because marketers have trained consumers not to trust advertising over the years. At one point, consumers thought they could use advertising as reliable information to make purchase decisions. Now, most ads are viewed with a cynical eye. Little boys who sent in their allowance for the Magic X-Ray Glasses advertised in the back of comic books are now grown men reading the fine print and looking for the way they're being tricked.

Another reason people are no longer as receptive to advertising is that too much of it is irrelevant to them. Interruptive marketing continues to erode in effectiveness, as consumers do not have time to filter all messages delivered to them to see which ones are applicable to them. Talking to people who are willing to listen is much more useful than forcing irrelevant messages on unwilling recipients. Effective advertisers aim the message to specific markets using targeted media placement.

Those specific markets are easier to reach than ever before. As mentioned in a previous chapter, the public has already sorted themselves into a diverse motley of distinctive groups. Just as individuals in those social groups are defined by similar cultural values and beliefs, they also share many of the same media consumption behaviors. Using that knowledge, brands can create a solid media placement plan that will make a well-designed ad even more effective.

The final tip for effective advertising is repetition. A good rule of thumb is that consumers will be exposed to your message three different times in three different media placements before they start to react to it. Smart media planners use the concepts of reach, the number of people that are exposed to your marketing messages, and frequency, the number of times those people hear the message, together to ensure that the message effectively gets to the largest number of people possible.

Reach and frequency must work together. Airing hundreds of ads (high frequency) on a radio station that no one listens to (low reach) will not be successful. Conversely, running one small ad for one day (low frequency) in the market's most popular newspaper (high reach) will also not deliver notable results.

Repetition of a clear authentic ad that is targeted to a relevant audience who is willing to listen can be one-step to incorporating the brand in the zeitgeist of the public. The important thing to remember about any advertising is that all ads, whether they are a part of a branding campaign or not, should consistently carry the brand's core attributes.

## The jolly old brand

Brands are a long-term proposition. Just a few ads or a couple of PR mentions won't have much effect over the short term. When you step back to look at brands that have used media and advertising over the long term, the power of a brand zeitgeist can clearly be seen.

The modern day image that most people have of Santa Claus, with the plump belly, red coat, and white beard has largely been shaped by media and advertising. For centuries, Santa Claus was portrayed as everything from a gnarled elf to a tall gaunt woodsman.

One of the first major steps to creating a unified Santa brand in the mind of the zeitgeist occurred with Clement Clark Moore's 1822 poem "A Visit From St. Nicholas" (commonly called "Twas the Night Before Christmas"). Moore's poem was published annually in numerous newspapers and periodicals and helped define the basic physical characteristics of Santa in the public's mind:

> Down the chimney St. Nicholas came with a bound.
> He was dressed all in fur, from his head to his foot,
> And his clothes were all tarnished with ashes and soot;
> A bundle of toys he had flung on his back,
> And he looked like a peddler just opening his pack.
> His eyes — how they twinkled! His dimples, how merry!
> His cheeks were like roses, his nose like a cherry!
> His droll little mouth was drawn up like a bow
> And the beard of his chin was as white as the snow;
> The stump of a pipe he held tight in his teeth,
> And the smoke it encircled his head like a wreath;
> He had a broad face and a little round belly,
> That shook when he laughed, like a bowlful of jelly.
> He was chubby and plump, a right jolly old elf,
> And I laughed when I saw him, in spite of myself;

In the latter part of the 19th century, cartoonist Thomas Nast built on the foundation of Moore's poem. He depicted Santa Claus as a plump man in a red suit and further cemented other aspects of the Santa brand in the zeitgeist with things such as a North Pole residency in his drawings for *Harper's Weekly* magazine.

The modern day image of Santa was firmly established starting in 1931 when Coca-Cola commissioned illustrator Haddon Sundblom to develop advertising images using Santa Claus. Sundblom further built on established canon by Moore and Nast and drew Santa as a warm and friendly human character. The Coca-Cola Santa was placed heavily in the company's annual Christmas ads in national magazines such as *The Saturday Evening Post, Ladies Home Journal, National Geographic, The New Yorker* and others.[22]

Santa Claus is a brand that reaches almost every section of the zeitgeist. Stop almost anyone on the street and they could recite a checklist of all of Santa's characteristics that have been established in the zeitgeist. If Santa is portrayed in the "wrong way," consumers will reject it — i.e. skinny in a blue suit. He's the ultimate example of a successful brand zeitgeist because everyone is on the same page as to what the brand represents.

*The modern day image of Santa Claus was established in the zeitgeist by media and marketing.*

However, there's no way you can replicate his success with your brand. For one thing, the media atmosphere is much different today. The entire populace isn't focused on a few big magazines and three television networks. You don't have Coca-Cola's media budget. You don't have two centuries to wait for your brand strategy to kick in. Finally, let's face it, you're not Santa Claus.

You can learn branding lessons from Santa on how to use media and messaging to establish your brand in the zeitgeist. Firstly, Santa has stayed true to a set of core brand assets and never drastically rebranded to keep up with trends and fads. During his busy season, he is everywhere. He's at the mall, in parades, on TV, in magazine ads, and in your house. The brand image is inescapable. The image is consistent, clear, and repeated to the point that the brand image of Santa Claus has been seared into mind's eye of the public.

The Santa Claus brand was spread in the zeitgeist over the long term by using traditional media and word-of-mouth. While it might be impossible to build a similar juggernaut brand using those same methods, there's now a new variable in the brand messaging and media equation. Until recently, Santa didn't have to deal with the Internet.

## Messaging through the digital zeitgeist

The most significant change in communication since Gutenberg's printing press has been the Internet. While the advent of mass media in the last century advanced the idea of immediate communication, the change that has occurred as a result of a digitally connected world over the past few decades is astounding. We are currently living in the days of a dramatic zeitgeist shift in media, advertising, and nearly every sector of business. As *Wired*'s Kevin Kelly wrote in a 2008 piece for the *New York Times Magazine*,

> "We are now in the middle of a second Gutenberg shift — from book fluency to screen fluency, from literacy to visuality." [23]

For years, businesses developed marketing and branding strategies that relied upon controlling a one-way message that went out to the market. With advances in technology and an interconnected audience, that message has become two-way and even multi-dimensional. It's no longer a message. It's a conversation.

That conversation is happening online between the brand and its audience. A discussion is also occurring between current customers, between satisfied customers and potential customers, and between disgruntled customers and potential customers. All these exchanges are happening in posts, tweets, and comments with or without the business being involved.

As a part of a sound business strategy, brands must learn to guide (not dictate) how these online messages are developed. They must be observant and reactive (or proactive) to what marketing messages are generated about them through online channels.

It's actually nothing new. These types of conversations have always occurred offline via word-of-mouth marketing. Now with new more efficient forms of communications, both positive and negative brand images can spread through the zeitgeist more quickly and with greater effect.

Some companies bemoan this development, because they feel they've lost control of their message. It's actually a huge opportunity. In the old model, an unhappy customer might tell several people about a bad experience and the company didn't know anything about it. Now in the new model, companies can actually monitor word-of-mouth interactions. If a customer is discontent and telling his social connections about it, the brand can step in to offer solutions by responding to the tweet, leaving a comment on their blog, or emailing the unhappy customer.

Still, many brands feel like they are facing a challenge with their online strategy. The technology evolves rapidly and when companies think they have established a solid strategy, the game changes. Companies were told they needed a web site. Then they needed a web store, then a blog, then a podcast, then a viral video, then user-generated content, then a social media presence. Now they need to embrace the mobile web and build an app. It never ends.

The key to growing a brand in the online zeitgeist is not to develop an online / new media strategy that relates to the current online trend / fad like building a Facebook page or getting a video to go viral, but to develop an overall new media philosophy. In general, that philosophy should be to stop thinking about online as a place for marketing messages because online is not a place to broadcast one-way messages. New media is actually a place to develop two-way customer service relationships.

# 8.

## Experiencing the Brand Relationship

Good marketing goes way beyond just getting customers in the door.

The customer experience should be an immense concern of the marketer and not just left to the operational side of the business. While advertising and other marketing may be promising one thing, the daily interactions in the business could be delivering another. The true indicator of brand success or failure hangs in the moments of interaction between the company and the consumer.

While some of those moments of contact happen via the marketing conversation through advertising, online networks, or other marketing messages, marketing is much more than just delivering messages to current and potential customers. Marketing has to follow through with the experience in order to build a long-term brand.

Escalating a brand to the point that it's well established with goodwill in the zeitgeist and delivering remarkable customer service are inseparable. Brands that enter the zeitgeist never do so with just marketing. No one ever pledged loyalty to a brand because they saw an advertisement. However, consumers do build strong and trusted relationships with brands because of the way the company treats them. Occasionally, it's just one exemplary situation that cements the goodwill, but sometimes it's the last minor straw in a negative experience that makes a consumer swear off the company forever.

It's usually the little things make the difference. Massive amounts of money in both marketing and product development are spent to convince consumers to choose one chain of gas stations over the competition. Eventually that investment gets a person standing in front of a gas pump. At some gas stations, instead of the grades of gas being presented on that pump low to high and cheap to expensive in a left to right pattern as people would expect, the most expensive grade is on the left in an attempt to trick the customer to accidentally select the higher priced gasoline. While it may provide a short-term revenue burst, tricking a customer is no way to establish a long-term relationship with your brand.

Companies can also choose to invest in their employees and create customer service philosophies that help to ensure a quality experience for their patrons. For example, a business could choose to spend money hiring additional personnel to handle incoming calls or purchase a telephone voice mail system that creates a maze for customers. Decisions made on the operational side of a business greatly affect the marketing effectiveness of building a brand in the zeitgeist. Customer service is not an expense. It's an investment in the brand.

An entrepreneur might spend loads of money on TV and radio commercials to publicize her restaurant. She purchases the best external signage to make sure people know where the restaurant is. She runs a full-page newspaper ad that includes a coupon.

The marketing works. Several patrons heard the broadcast spots. Quite a few people cut out and use the coupon. Some people drove by, saw the sign, and decided to try the restaurant.

However, as those people arrived, they found that there was a long unnecessary wait to get a table. The baked potatoes were raw in the middle. The waiter was rude. People saw the bottoms of their coffee cups and tea glasses too many times. The restrooms were dirty. Suddenly, all of the entrepreneur's marketing investment was wasted. The marketing did sell one meal to those customers, but the brand was forever damaged with the experience. Those people probably won't be back and will spread negative reactions in the zeitgeist to their social groups.

Brands are built with positive one-on-one relations with customers. Sub par customer experiences can stifle any potential the brand had to spread in the zeitgeist. Most importantly, damaging negative customer experiences sometimes spread faster than the brand building ones. Exact statistics vary depending on the industry and the survey process. However, on average, studies show people share good consumer experiences with one or two people while bad experiences are related to seven to nine people.

## A positive brand zeitgeist is embedded in employees

It's one thing to have talking points and mission statements that say the brand is dedicated to customer service. It's quite another to follow through on that promise. One company that has built a zeitgeist brand using the power of the positive customer experience is Zappos.

Zappos is an online retailer that sells shoes, handbags, and other apparel accessories. While selling a relatively routine product line, Zappos has created a remarkable customer experience around the shoe purchasing transaction. Tony Hsieh, the CEO of Zappos, has said that while he and the other company founders were in the early stages of building the brand, they decided, "We're a service company that just happens to sell shoes."[24] It's an important distinction that helps set the company apart from competitors who are taking notes from the Zappos customer service philosophy that is centered on their employees.

"Customer service is not just something you stick up on a plaque in the lobby," Aaron Magness, business development director at Zappos declared. "You have to be willing to hire and fire for those values. Customer service cannot be taught. It has to be innate in the employee."[25]

Zappos carefully interviews potential hires to ensure that they fit the company culture. All employees, regardless of position, are required to take a month long training course, which includes at least two weeks of working in the call center talking on the phone with actual customers.

After a week of this training, the new employee is offered the "Quit Now Bonus," their full week of salary for the time they've worked plus an additional $2000 — no strings attached. Zappos says this is to ensure that people are truly dedicated to the brand culture and not just there for a paycheck. Around 97% of new hires reject the buyout.[26]

This hiring process protects the Zappos brand. If a company's brand is deeply rooted in the company culture, then disturbances to that culture can affect the brand. Magness says that Zappos employees are some of the best guardians of the Zappos brand culture. The employees contribute annually to the Zappos "Culture Book" which describes what the company culture means to them.

*Zappos has built a successful brand using exemplary customer service and employee empowerment.*

Some business leaders might look at the Zappos model and see a bunch of new-age feel-good gobbledygook that really doesn't work. It's because they've seen too many companies try to force an artificial company culture with compulsory team building exercises, retreats, and motivational posters. Employees reject the culture because they know it's only skin-deep and doesn't really affect the way that the company relates to employees and, in turn, how those employees treat customers. The Zappos model proves the employment empowerment model works because they actually mean it when they empower their employees.

Brands are relationships and those relationships with consumers start inside with your employees. All external brand marketing will be for naught if an unhappy, unappreciated, or uninformed employee delivers a sub par customer experience. Brands that want to spread their message in the zeitgeist must invest in their staff and empower them to make the right brand decisions when dealing with clients. This involves communicating the basic brand strategy to each employee as well as letting employees know how important they are to the overall brand.

## Empowering employees to build the brand

Empowering employees to create extraordinary customer service can plant brand zeitgeist seeds that sprout in unexpected places in both traditional word-of-mouth channels and in online spaces. In 2007, a Zappos customer purchased a pair of shoes for her mother. The shoes didn't fit and she was going to ship them back (which is always free from Zappos), but her mother passed away. In the following chaotic days, the woman forgot about the shoes. She wrote a blog post that detailed her experience with Zappos:

> When I came home this last time, I had an email from Zappos asking about the shoes, since they hadn't received them. I was just back and not ready to deal with that, so I replied that my mom had died but that I'd send the shoes as soon as I could. They emailed back that they had arranged

with UPS to pick up the shoes, so I wouldn't have
to take the time to do it myself. I was so touched.
That's going against corporate policy.
Yesterday, when I came home from town, a florist
delivery man was just leaving. It was a beauti-
ful arrangement in a basket with white lilies and
roses and carnations. Big and lush and fragrant. I
opened the card, and it was from Zappos. I burst
into tears. I'm a sucker for kindness, and if that
isn't one of the nicest things I've ever had happen
to me, I don't know what is.[27]

This story could have easily been written from the viewpoint
of an angry customer who was lashing out at a company for being
insensitive and uncaring. I'm positive there's not a section in the
Zappos operations manual that details how to send flowers to
a customer who forgets to send shoes back because her mother
dies. Nevertheless, the Zappos culture empowers their employees
to not only do the right thing (extending the return time), but to
go beyond the right thing (arranging the UPS pickup), and then
to occasionally go to extraordinary service levels (the flowers).

It paid off. Normally, this story would have just created one
lifelong dedicated fan of the brand, which is a valuable commodity in itself. This particular blog post has spread virally around the
web and provided an incalculable boost in positive karma in the
zeitgeist for Zappos.[28]

## Good is great. Bad is worse.

Unfortunately for brands (and consumers), these encour-
aging customer service stories happen, or perhaps are reported,
fewer times than the incredible instances when customer service
dramatically fails. United Airlines learned how the entire image
of the brand could be damaged when one customer is unhappy.

Dave Carroll is a member of the Canadian musical group, Sons of Maxwell. While on tour, he flew on United Airlines from Halifax to a show in Nebraska. Carroll alleges that he and other passengers watched as baggage handlers carelessly tossed his guitar case while the plane was on a stopover at Chicago's O'Hare. When he arrived at his destination, he discovered his expensive Taylor guitar had been significantly damaged.

Carroll says he began a year long saga of fruitless communication with United about the incident beginning immediately after the incident with flight attendants in Chicago and ending with someone at United Airlines corporate offices that Carroll refers to as Ms. Irlweg who told him that the final word from the airline was no.

He says he was pushed from person to person at United with each person saying it wasn't his or her problem. In their last communication, Carroll told Irlweg that he would write and release three songs with music videos about how he thought the airline treated him poorly.

The first song was entitled "United Breaks Guitars" and achieved nearly 3 million views within the first few weeks of being posted on YouTube in the summer of 2009. The story was also featured in several newspapers and on several major TV networks. The song was released and heavily downloaded on iTunes. The YouTube version of the United song has now been viewed over 6 million times.[29]

The incident became a public relations nightmare for United. Some analysts even tied the song to a concurrent 10% dip in the airline's stock price that equated to a decline of $180 million in shareholder value.[30] While some dispute the stock fact, it is a fact that the song has become a permanent black eye in the zeitgeist for the United brand.

In the first few days after the release of the video, United contacted Carroll and offered compensation for the guitar. He refused, stating that he had already tried to resolve the matter and that he would continue with the other two songs. He said the airline could give the money to charity if they wished and United donated $3,000 to a musical institute.

Carroll has said that the employees he dealt with at United including Ms. Irlweg were kind and unflappable, but were just upholding flawed customer service policies.[31] He hopes that United will change their customer service policy as a result of the videos. It looks like they might. United has started using the song and video in internal employee training.[32]

## The online customer relationship

Accompanied by a reflective mirror-like cover in 2006, Time Magazine declared that its annual Person of the Year was "You" in response to how the Internet had now enabled a new online community of collaboration and helped create an influx of user-generated content like blogs, YouTube videos, and other consumer created media.

> "The new Web is a very different thing. It's a tool for bringing together the small contributions of millions of people and making them matter. Silicon Valley consultants call it Web 2.0, as if it were a new version of some old software. But it's really a revolution." [33]

This revolution of individuals becoming micropublishers is one that brands need to watch and understand as they attempt to build a brand. Brands now exist in an environment where a single blog post, tweet, or online video can either help or destroy a brand's position in the zeitgeist.

*Time magazine's 2006 Person of the Year was "You".*

Whether it's a positive brand boost like the blog post of the satisfied Zappos' customer or the brand-damaging debacle of the United Breaks Guitars song trilogy, it's easy to see that the customer service relationship has now been extended to the interactive online realm. As mentioned in an earlier chapter, today's online environment is not a place to transmit a one-way message. New media is actually a place to develop a customer service relationship.

Just as you would expect a company to proactively deal with angry or dissatisfied customers who physically come into a real world store, brands should proactively deal with disgruntled customers online as well. Companies should monitor what is being said about them in cyberspace and step into volatile situations in an attempt to resolve the problem or placate the frustrated customer.

Don't despair. The opportune thing is that the online community who has taken control of your brand is not completely an angry mob. There are genuine fans of the brand who want to be brand ambassadors, and companies should help them do that for two major reasons. Firstly, online consumers who are brand advocates are closer to what's actually happening out in the real world. They can react for the brand in places where the brand might not be able to go. The other reason is that the brand message is much more authentic coming from fellow consumers.

Tightly controlling the brand message is not an option, and frankly, never has been an option even prior to the Internet. In essence, the online consumers who are now taking a part in the brand's messaging are nothing more than a more potent version of traditional word-of-mouth. However, instead of just sharing word-of-mouth with their immediate social circles, they can now broadcast their praises and complaints to the entire world.

So just as companies expect their employees to be brand ambassadors, consumers now also have the power to be brand advocates. As brands provide internal brand guidelines to employees, companies now should learn to guide and help these "citizen marketers" as well. The single most effective long-term marketing strategy is to grow a base of dedicated loyal users.

One of the most popular public profile pages on Facebook with over 4 million fans is dedicated to Coca-Cola. Except the Coke page wasn't created by Coca-Cola.

The page was created by two Coke fans in Los Angeles, Dusty Sorg and Michael Jedrzejewski, just because they enjoyed the brand. Instead sending of a cease and desist order, Coca Cola worked with Facebook to contact the cola enthusiasts. They invited them to the brand's world headquarters in Atlanta for VIP treatment and meetings to discuss how the brand could collaborate with them to manage the page.[34]

What else could they do? If they had bullied the original page creators for ownership, they would have lost the admiration of two of their biggest brand advocates as well as hurt their reputation with the millions of fans who had joined the page. It would have been akin to the major league baseball player refusing to sign an autograph for a 10-year-old fan who adores him.

Looking back at the history of traditional media and customer relations, would Coca-Cola have let two fans create, design, and direct the 'I'd like to buy the world a Coke" commercial? It would have been unthinkable. However, customer service and the brand experience have been changed forever. The customer and brand relationship is now multi-dimensional with both parties leading and following at the same time.

# 9.

## Bottom Line Brands

Marketing is part art — part science. The scientific part is easy to measure with plenty of numbers like audience size, budgets, and sales. Branding makes up large piece of the art part. The problem is how do you measure a relationship?

There is a direct correlation between strong brand-consumer relationships and increased revenues. However, it may not be an immediate correlation. Even if you develop a brand that has permeated the zeitgeist and is top-of-mind in the market, you still have to wait until someone is ready to buy. That time lag is what makes branding so hard to measure.

Since 1953, Chevrolet and Corvette fans have established the Corvette in the zeitgeist as "America's Sports Car." In any given year, part of Chevrolet's marketing budget included Corvette branding elements that might have caused some 16-year-old boy to start lusting after the sports car. Over the next several years, he notices every Corvette he sees on the road. He reads car magazine articles about the Corvette. He joins the Corvette's Facebook page. When the man is thirty-four, a local Chevy dealer runs a special financing promotion that prompts him to finally purchase a Corvette. To which marketing budget and activity do you credit the sale?

The answer is all of them. The man had always had a relationship with the Corvette brand even though he had never purchased the car. Had Chevrolet never built a strong brand before he first became interested or let their heritage brand drop out of the zeitgeist over the intervening eighteen years, he might have lost interest. Eventually, the dealership initiated the direct call-to-action that closed the sale.

The waiting is the hardest part for brands. Most companies don't have eighteen years to wait before their marketing efforts kick in. They need revenue now. Of course, that's the way most marketing is designed. It directly asks the consumer to make the purchase decision now.

The branding portion of the marketing plan should always be running in the background as a fundamental part of the organization's day-to-day marketing and operations. For example, the brand's core assets should consistently be presented in those direct advertising and PR messages. The company should continuously build relationships with consumers through positive customer experiences with the brand. Brands should be proactive in reacting to problems that threaten the brand. It's a simple case of simultaneously maintaining what is there and growing into new areas.

## You can't manage what you can't measure

But is the branding working right now? How can companies measure the effectiveness of their marketing efforts to promote the intangible aspects of the brand into the zeitgeist?

In the late 1800s, a man named John Wanamaker in Philadelphia opened one of the first department stores in the United States. He was a pioneer in retail marketing and is credited with many retail innovations.[35] Wanamaker is also recognized as originating one of marketing's most famous axioms:

"Half the money I spend on advertising is wasted; the trouble is, I don't know which half."

*Retail mogul John Wanamaker declared that he didn't
know which half of his marketing was working.*

While this quote is still used today to justify marketing
expenditures, the truth is we've come a long way in the ability
to track marketing ROI since Mr. Wanamaker was in business.
If you don't know what half of your marketing is working, then
you need to stop marketing because you're wasting money, time,
consumer attention, and brand equity.

Specific marketing campaigns are reasonably easy to track
since there are clear numbers in investment, the size of the market, and the resulting sales. Branding is a bit harder to measure
as it is intangible, but it's still possible to see what's working by
measuring the opinion of the zeitgeist.

Brands can be evaluated across three broad metrics: perception, performance, and value.

Within the perception metric are concepts such as brand
awareness, recall, and recognition. Brand awareness is the simple
test of finding out if consumers know the brand exists. Without
brand awareness, nothing else will work. Recall and recognition
measure marketing effectiveness by the ability of consumers to
recall or recognize names, logos, or other brand assets. Perception

also looks at what attributes consumers assign to brands such as credibility, quality, and relevance.

Brands can be measured by performance of their customers in areas such as brand loyalty and preference. Will consumers seek the brand out over another similar option? Will they pay a premium price for it? Are consumers who are brand advocates able to convey the brand story to other consumers? Is sufficient positive word-of-mouth occurring with the brand? Is the brand gaining new loyal customers?

Lastly, to get a big picture idea of how the brand is faring, you can estimate the overall monetary value of the brand by looking at how much another corporation would be willing to pay for the entire brand on the open market. When you take that price and subtract inventory, real estate, and other tangible assets, you are left with the value of the intangible aspects of the brand. After accounting for inflation and other external factors, you can use this value to track the progression or regression of the equity a brand has in the market over time.

Many of these metrics require extensive research or number crunching. However, there's an easy way to get a quick thumbnail view of the value of a brand. Just measure the difference between the generic and the branded.

You can make yourself a cup of coffee at home for a pittance or you can pay a premium price to have a barista make you some in a Starbucks cup. The value that Starbucks adds to the basic commodity of coffee is the essence of their brand. Sure, some of that increase in value is because of Starbucks' basic overhead expenses of doing it for you as well as the value of the professional equipment and expertise used to brew the coffee. However, most of the increase in value over the home brewed cup exists in what the zeitgeist thinks about what the logo on the cup represents.

Starbucks wasn't able to charge a premium price for coffee overnight. It took years of careful manipulation of their image and millions of coffee purchase transactions to establish what they are. Over those years, their customers developed a lifestyle around the brand which is now firmly ingrained in the zeitgeist. In the end, all those strategies, interactions, and experiences have enabled Starbucks to use their brand to influence their bottom line.

# *Conclusion*

A Chinese proverb says the best time to plant a tree was 20 years ago, but the second best time to plant one is today.

Just as it takes time to have the ability to stand under the shade of a fully developed tree; it takes time to build a brand. If a company doesn't have a brand strategy, they need one today.

That brand strategy should consider the zeitgeist and how it constantly evolves. People influence the direction of the zeitgeist and the zeitgeist influences the direction of brands. Brands should take into consideration how people think, why they act like they do, how they relate to one another, why they align themselves with certain groups, and why they share information with their peers.

When a brand image is formulated that fits into those people's worldview, the actual tactics for marketing become easier and more effective. Building a trusted relationship with a group of dedicated consumers and guiding the conversation with them are the fundamental keys to success of embedding a brand in the zeitgeist.

# About the Author

Chris Houchens is a marketing speaker, writer, blogger, and consultant. He has spent years working in both media and marketing including as the operations manager of a radio group, as the online director of a newspaper, and as the marketing director of a healthcare organization.

Houchens is a dynamic marketing speaker traveling worldwide delivering marketing keynotes and other presentations to conferences and corporate events.

Chris' blog, the Shotgun Marketing Blog, offers common sense insights on marketing and has been ranked as a top marketing blog.

Houchens has been the co-author and reviewer of several marketing books and is also a contributing writer and source for numerous online and print publications.

Chris is a past president of the Professional Marketing Association and was honored as that organization's 2007 Marketer of the Year. He was privileged to have been selected as a Forum Fellow for the Louisville Courier-Journal. He serves as a volunteer for several non-profit organizations and has served on several non-profit boards as a marketing advisor.

Read the Shotgun Marketing Blog at www.ShotgunConcepts.com or find out how to bring Chris to speak to your group at www.ChrisHouchens.com.

Follow him on Twitter at @shotgunconcepts.

# Connect Online

Visit www.BrandZeitgeist.com to continue the conversation. You'll find the author's Shotgun Marketing blog as well as opportunities to connect with Brand Zeitgeist through Twitter, Facebook, and other forms of social media.

# *Brand Examples*

Several brands have been used as examples in this book. Most are listed below. All brands used as examples in this book should not be taken as endorsements or disparagements of these companies or entities.

Abercrombie and Fitch
Alka-Seltzer
American Express
Apple
Avon Skin So Soft
Barack Obama
Charmin
Chevrolet Corvette
Chicago Cubs
Chrysler
Coca-Cola
Digital Equipment Corporation
Duncan Hines
Dyson Vacuums
Facebook
Ford
General Motors
Google
Grateful Dead
Hawaii
Hummer

IKEA
Kentucky
Kentucky Fried Chicken (KFC)
Kleenex
Levis
Michael Jackson
Microsoft Windows
Mountain Dew
MTV
Old Spice
Pepsi
PETA
Proctor and Gamble
Ruth's Chris Steakhouse
Santa Claus
Saturday Night Live
Seven-Up
Southwest Airlines
SPAM (Hormel)
Star Trek
Starbucks
Tropicana
Twitter
United Airlines
Wayne Gretzky
Whole Foods
Xerox
Y2K
Zappos
Numerous other general industry examples

# References / Notes

[1]  "Google Press Center: Zeitgeist." www.google.com/zeitgeist (accessed December 20, 2009).

[2]  "Google Flu Trends." www.google.org/flutrends (accessed on December 20, 2009).

[3]  "Kentucky Unbridled Spirit." kentucky.gov/Pages/unbridledspirit (accessed on December 20, 2009).

[4]  "Louis Cheskin, 72; Studied motivation and effects of color." The New York Times, October 10, 1981.

[5]  Gladwell, Malcolm. Blink. New York: Little, Brown and Co., 2005.

[6]  Helm, Burt. "Blowing Up Pepsi." Businessweek, April 23, 2009.

[7]  Abend, Lisa. "The Font War: IKEA fans fume over Verdana." Time. http://www.time.com/time/business/article/0,8599,1919127,00.html (accessed on December 20, 2009).

[8]  Koenigs, M. and D. Tranel. "Prefrontal cortex damage abolishes brand-cued changes in cola preference." Social Cognitive and Affective Neuroscience 3(2008).

[9]  Maslow, A.H. "The Theory of Human Motivation." Psychological Review, 50.4 (1943): 370–396.

[10]  "McDonald's Test Markets Spam." Pacific Business News (Honolulu), June 11, 2002.

[11]  Rosenfield, Jill. "CDU to Gretzky: The Puck Stops Here!" Fast Company 36, June 2000.

[12]  Mikkelson, Barbara and David. "Ken Olsen Computer Quote." www.snopes.com/quotes/kenolsen.asp (accessed on December 20, 2009).

[13]  "Detroit: Same Old, Same Old." National Review, November 16, 2008.

[14] "Old Spice does new tricks." Brandweek, June, 2, 2003.
[15] Cheung, Melissa. "Hormel Fights for Spam Name." CBS News. http://www.cbsnews.com/stories/2003/07/30/tech/main565821.shtml (accessed on December 20, 2009).
[16] Miller, Claire Cain. "Twitter Serves Up Ideas From Its Followers." New York Times, October 25, 2009.
[17] Holy Bible. King James Version. Revelation Chapter 3 verses 16-17.
[18] Hall, Steve. "Southwest Airlines Gets Its Rap on With Rapping Flight Attendant." http://www.adrants.com/2009/03/southwest-airlines-gets-its-rap-on-with.php (accessed on December 20, 2009).
[19] "The Mojave Experiment." Microsoft Corporation. http://www.microsoft.com/windows/windows-vista/mojave.aspx (accessed on December 20, 2009).
[20] Manjoo, Farhad. "Vista Revisited." Slate. http://www.slate.com/id/2207756/ (accessed on December 20, 2009).
[21] Schwartz, Barry. The Paradox of Choice. New York: Harper Collins. 2004."
[22] "Santa Coke Lore." The Coca-Cola Company. http://www.the-coca-colacompany.com/heritage/cokelore_santa.html (accessed on December 20, 2009).
[23] Kelly, Kevin. "Idea Lab: Becoming Screen Literate." The New York Times Magazine, November 23, 2008: MM48.
[24] Chafkin, Max. "How I Did It: Tony Hsieh, CEO, Zappos.com." Inc Magazine, September 1, 2006.
[25] Magness, Aaron (Zappos). Telephone interview by Chris Houchens, February 2009.
[26] McFarland, Keith. "Why Zappos Offers New Hires $2,000 to Quit." BusinessWeek, September 16, 2008.
[27] "I heart Zappos." http://www.zazlamarr.com/blog/?p=240 (accessed on February 15, 2009).
[28] Godin, Seth. Blog. http://sethgodin.typepad.com/seths_blog/2007/10/do-you-think-th.html (posted on October 16, 2007).
[29] Carroll, Dave. "United Breaks Guitars." http://www.youtube.com/watch?v=5YGc4zOqozo (accessed on December 20, 2009).

[30] Ayres, Chris. "Revenge is best served cold" The TimesOnline (London), July 22, 2009.

[31] Carroll, Dave. "Statement." http://www.youtube.com/watch?v=T_X-Qoh_mw (accessed on December 20, 2009).

[32] "Broken guitar song gets airline's attention." Canadian Broadcasting Corporation, July 8, 2009.

[33] "Person of the Year: You." Time Magazine, December 13, 2006.

[34] "Coke's Facebook Page." Advertising Age. http://adage.com/digital/article?article_id=135238 (accessed June 13, 2009).

[35] "The Advertising Century". Advertising Age, December 1999.

# Bring Brand Zeitgeist to you

Bring the author of Brand Zeitgeist, Chris Houchens, to speak at your event.

Chris Houchens delivers an experience that the attendees at your event will be motivated by and can implement when they get back to the office. Chris' presentations are entertaining and informative. His marketing knowledge is delivered in a sensible down-to-earth style that is well received by your audience. It's a message that's straight to the point, clearly presented, and full of takeaways. Each presentation, which is customized for your audience, is infused with energy, humor, and real world examples.

*Bring the author of this book, Chris Houchens, to speak at your event.*

Chris has a special presentation focusing on the ideas of the Brand Zeitgeist, but also has other presentations across a wide array of business and marketing topics. For a full list of these topics as well as testimonials from past audiences, and more information about a personal appearance or keynote presentation, visit www.ChrisHouchens.com.